Becky,
Best wishes for many laughs and good times!
Blake

THE GHOST OF PORNOS PAST

Humorous Prose

COMIC
SEQUENTIAL
STORIES

THE GHOST OF PORNOS PAST

BLAKE
RICHARDS

CREATIVE INTANGIBLES, INC.
SAUGERTIES, NEW YORK

Printed in the United States of America

Creative Intangibles, Inc.
P.O. Box 38
Saugerties, New York 12477-0038
www.CreativeIntangibles.com

Cover design, illustrations and author photo: Charlene Rettew

Library of Congress Control Number: 2003097332
ISBN: 0-9745678-0-9

First Edition

For my parents

PREFACE

The punctuation of words I wrote with unusual forms or usage dotted the book's double-page spreads like bikini-wax bumps on thighs with text tattoos. Imagining how that might appear if a reader were to use a string bookmark, I decided against those grammatical highlights.

Although the following stories can exist independently, this book is structured to be read sequentially.

Enjoy,
Blake

CONTENTS

Whorehouse Forklift Operators Needed

Whorehouse Forklift Operators Needed

"What do you eat before going to a brothel?" Dave wondered as he and Sam drove into Reno.

"Do you think we'll ever come back?" Sam asked.

Dave pondered this question and its relevance to their dining decision. They pulled into an all-you-can-eat truck stop buffet, certain to be dining among other brothel patrons. Their questions of prostitution's and gambling's value to the community were answered by the plethora of fortified pawn shops. They joked about writing a letter to the mayor recommending a municipal name change to Desperation, Nevada but figured he'd probably already pawned his tenure.

Before breaking to eat, Dave and Sam had perused a couple of the shops. They saw the usual pawned items: watches, jewelry, leather jackets, guns, but these shops were unforgettably unique for their more tragic items. On display were prostheses, retainers, hairpieces, and even a pacemaker, each with a powerful story eagerly told by an indifferent shop owner. Take the man who'd handed over his prosthetic leg and hopped out of the store with a smile on his face, feeling he'd gotten the better of the deal. Even though he'd given up a ten thousand dollar prosthetic for four hundred bucks, he'd left happy, knowing that had he not sold the leg and come up with the money the leg would have been broken. Most customers exited with similar parting words, "I think I feel a streak coming on!"

At the buffet table, Dave glanced under the heat lamps to determine what he'd consume next. It felt like roulette; he knew he'd pick something but wouldn't leave feeling like a winner. Looking around at the patrons he noticed a universal affliction — they didn't know when to walk away.

Sam and Dave talked strategy, mapping out their game plan for both buffet and brothel with intense precision. Inspired, Sam even contemplated opening his own B&B, figuring these combined services would be cost-effective, as both involved cheap pieces of meat kept warm by artificial lighting. Also, each entailed making a selection that, hopefully, wouldn't leave you feeling funny when you went to the bathroom.

Sam told of his old mentor, Sitz, who was no stranger to brothels decades ago. Listening, Dave swelled with sentimentality as he felt there was something especially precious about hearing stories and advice passed from mentor to protégé. Sitz had briefed Sam about the prostitute who'd been head choreographer for the Radio City Music Hall farmclub, the Reno Rockettes. She did away with the traditional, high leg kicks for fear of bursting an implant and instituted, instead, chorus-line routines of synchronized mooning. Also, Sitz had instructed, "Ask the madam to see their time cards — always be sure to steer clear of those trying to pull a double shift." Sam and Dave put on their poker faces and headed for the car.

Driving east out of Reno, the car was eerily quiet as Dave became more apprehensive about letting Sam talk him into this venture. Dave drove; Sam clutched tightly a detailed map of the brothel zone he'd downloaded from the Internet. They were going in old-school, no fancy car computer system connecting them with an operator outlining the most efficient route. Although, Sam thought it would be more fun talking to an Onstar representative who would be obliged to listen to the details of their vacation itinerary.

Dave could smell sleaze in the air; he knew they were close. Sam broke the silence, "Do you think we'll recognize anyone? Maybe former Governor Jesse Ventura?"

"If we recognize anyone," Dave said, "it'll be our high-school chemistry teacher." This rouge educator had bragged at their graduation about inventing the perfect pill for perverts, claiming it had greater vascular power than Viagra, was superior to penicillin, and even managed to repel cheap perfume from one's skin. After a short stint with Merck, their management, not recognizing his brilliance, had left him independent in the Nevada hills.

Sam, moments earlier, had been afflicted by a rare, desert allergy attack leaving him shaking and snorting. He and Dave were feeling more like Beavis and Butthead than the upstanding citizens they envisioned themselves to be. Dave tried to rationalize, "We're only patronizing the world's oldest profession." Silence followed, as both realized their rationalizations would best be left for afterwards.

"What are you going to do?" Dave asked.

"Whatever I can get the best deal on," Sam said.

Dave pulled into a parking space at the brothel but for unknown reasons left the car running. To their side was a dumpster and beside it, a green recycling bin labeled "Douche Bags." They were both pleased to see the girls' earth-friendly attitude. Dave speculated *Hozone* might be an organization of prostitutes for saving the atmosphere.

This brothel's sales pitch was clear; Dave and Sam sat dazed as it certainly wasn't aesthetics. They absorbed the view of what appeared to be a post-apocalyptic, glorified trailer complex that looked like compound headquarters for some group of blind supremacists.

Once inside, the pair stood in the gathering room as a dozen, cosmetically mismatched women assembled before them. While these ladies had been filing in, Dave was consumed by a sense of grandeur. Nobility fantasies rushed to his head. These elated feelings were soon replaced by the sobering reality of not-dim-enough lighting. Instead of conjuring Ceasaresque thoughts, Dave now embodied the mentality of a Popeyes' overnight manager.

"That must be the Maaa..Dam," Sam stuttered, his voice ending with a sense of shock and a discernible tinge of fear.

The stereotypical madam strode toward them. Under a different set of circumstances, both instinctually would have been inclined to run. A lady of proportions, so generous as to be deserving of the Nobel Peace Prize, now stood before them. Had Nelson Mandella joined them, he obviously would have bowed his head in defeat. Had Jimmy Carter accompanied them, Dave still would have had to drive. In a ceremony that now reminded him of the opening proceedings to Bob Barker's lifelong dream of hosting an erotic version of "The Price is Right," the madam commenced with the introductions.

Dave was momentarily distracted by an enormous trophy sitting atop the cash register. At first glance it looked like a bowling award with a woman bent, beginning to bowl. Soon though, he noticed the figure standing behind her, and clearly the man wasn't her coach.

A Japanese man, whose company had recently relocated him to Reno, entered tentatively and bowed repeatedly to the madam. She was uncertain whether the man could speak English and wondered if this was just a polite greeting or an indication that he wanted oral sex. Having just returned from an Asian brothel book tour for her bestseller, *The 30 Second Manager,* the madam prepared to check her pocket translator. Fortunately, in perfect English, the man offered, "I'll pay you 10,000 yen to walk through my house with your shoes on."

After agreeing in Japanese, the madam proceeded with the introductions. Her words echoed through the brothel, "That's Cinnamon. Next to her is the lovely and sultry Ginger."

Observing Ginger, a wrestling referee announced in Dave's head, "Hailing from and with parts unknown."

The ladies names were primarily spices or pieces of medical equipment. They were all the usual spices except for a woman called Anise. During the announcements it was common to hear their career highlights, sexual milestones, technical specialties and celebrity encounters. One not only was the current title-holder for the world's biggest areola, but also claimed a rendezvous with Gary Coleman. Another was the currently reigning Miss Nude Montana From The Knees Down.

Dave and Sam glanced at each other, simultaneously contemplating the madam's work history and, more importantly, her present work status. These days she could turn two tricks at once with the johns never meeting.

At the bar sat two customers dining on Viagra from a pretzel bowl, struggling to make idle chat. Outside of a women's golf clubhouse, you'd rarely hear conversation this strained. During one of the excruciatingly long quiet spells, the one man dropped his business card into the raffle fishbowl sitting on the bar. At the end of every month, one brazen fellow would get a call at the workplace announcing his free handjob.

Contemplating his form of payment, Dave recalled the credit card ad he'd seen on an adult cable channel: "At the world-famous Snatchman, Jackinoff and Clitorstein Brothel in Nevada they'll take it in the ass, but they won't take American Express. Visa — it's everywhere you want to be peed on!" Dave stood there checking his wallet and absorbing the environment, while tuning out the insincere compliments that had been flying his way since the introductions.

Sam's physiology began to change. Dave couldn't evaluate it, so he ignored it. "Beth," Dave said, happily choosing a lady with an outside-the-profession name. Beth began to walk towards him, clearly pleased not to have ended up with Sam who now was starting to twitch. Thinking Sam was reverting to his high-school excitement levels, Dave disregarded his behavior, then realized something was going on. Sam wasn't turning into The Incredible Hulk, and surely nothing was going to tear through his clothes, yet something strange was occurring. Suddenly it hit Dave! Sam was experiencing the severe onset of T&A

Induced High Roller syndrome. Clinically, this condition is characterized as the delusioned inflation of one's monetary and social stature resulting from over-exposure to female sexuality.

Not certain how to properly intervene, Dave knew he would have to quickly improvise. In a spontaneous effort to save Sam's finances from certain peril, he blurted futilely, "Cinnamon!" Sam indiscriminately proceeded to add three other girls to Dave's altruistic decision.

Now fully symptomatic of the condition, Sam was in danger of being deemed under the influence of PCP. The brothel owner, who was clutching what seemed to be a useless, oversized dildo, relaxed as he and the madam acknowledged that instead of having a crazed drugee on their hands, they had a crazed spender. The owner, who had been overseeing renovations to reinforce the platform behind a wooly, mechanical-bull version of the shepard's friend, was now intent on capitalizing on Sam's compromised state.

Noticing the attire of one of Sam's girls, Dave recalled Sitz's story about the prostitute who got crabs so often she had to wear fishnet panties. Again trying to intervene, Dave said, "He's, ah special," as the owner whisked Sam and his four companions to the VIP suite. Dave's attempt at temporary guardianship had failed, and Sam would go on to empty his wallet not only of the past-expiration-date condom which he had optimistically transferred from one worn-out wallet to the next, but also of all his cash, travelers checks, and steakhouse gift certificates. The madam swiped his credit cards as if she were fifteen and working her first day as a cashier, had a cereal-box bar code that wouldn't register but was too nervous to call for a price check.

As Beth and Dave proceeded to Beth's room, he paused in the lobby to glance at the bulletin board. Absent were the customary bulletin postings: lost cats, timeshares, guitar lessons. In their place was an open call to men who wanted to partake in a subtitled, blooper porn movie; a fifty-count box of thongs, described "as is"; and a "seeking worldly retiree" notice, clearly devoid of any transparent intention.

Passing the housekeeping cart, Dave realized that all clients must leave feeling better about their occupation. As they continued down the hall, Dave tried not to stare at Beth's colossally collagened lips. He wondered if their extreme augmentation was intentional so they could function as shock absorbers when she was giving head.

Pausing at the door to Beth's room, his reservations returned. He struggled to devise a tactful extraction from the pending interaction. Entering, Dave was overcome by still-fresh Scotchguard fumes. He flashed back to years earlier, when as a struggling waiter in LA he'd taken a job Scotchguarding sofas in the San Fernando Valley. Having become overly sensitized to the chemical from his time on the job, Dave began feeling slightly light-headed as he started to sit in the lone vinyl chair. Instantly, he found himself on the floor staring at his dazed image in the ceiling mirrors. Having been in the Scotchguarding business, he should have foreseen the over-application miscalculation which had coated the vinyl chair like a buttered casserole dish.

Not knowing whether he was seeing four of himself due to cheap mirror installation or neurological damage, panic ensued. As Dave lay there in pain, his first impulse, which he luckily curtailed, was to scream for his mother. Worried how he would financially survive with brain injury, Dave's thoughts turned to litigation. He wondered, "How do I get in touch with a lawyer now?" Thinking better of asking for a phonebook or trying to recall a catchy radio commercial, he realized he should get a recommendation.

Still slightly delirious from the fall, paranoia set in. Dave feared that the owner, concerned about liability, might send in the madam to sit on his face until he ran out of air. After this queening, they would administer large doses of Viagra and chalk it up as just another overdose.

In the VIP suite Sam laughed regally. He had assumed Robin Leach mannerisms and was telling bad jokes. The boisterous chatter subdued only long enough to differentiate the intercom announcement. "Code Red, Code Red, Code Red!" a wet voice cried out. Assuming this was a notification of his presence, Sam paused momentarily to savor the moment.

Dave had stopped breathing and began to turn blue. Panicking and returning from the intercom announcement, Beth wondered if she had called in the right code. Back on the intercom Beth yelled, "Code Blue, Code Blue, Code Blue," remembering that red was if you'd recognized a family member. She now knelt by Dave's aqua face. Trained in the correction of blue balls, she proceeded to remove his unit. Thinking a blowjob would resuscitate him, Beth desperately tried to perform, frantically transferring from one position to the next, all to no avail. Her recently re-enlarged breasts pressed firmly against the floor, keeping her head inches from Dave's penis. Grasping the immediate urgency, Beth tried tirelessly. Each time her head and body bounced back against her weighted thrust as if riding a pogo stick. With 48 triple-G's preventing her misplaced, resuscitation attempt, Beth resorted to just holding Dave's penis firmly with both hands, recalling a "Cops" episode where someone kept yelling, "Support the head, support the head!"

By this time, Sam was shirtless; unfortunately for the ladies, it revealed his Robin Leach physique. He hollered and hooted as the girls' actions became more frenzied.

Miraculously Dave came to. As a result of his head swinging back violently and hitting the floor, some hallucinations were bound to arise. First, there could be no explanation to the Denny's waitress steadily bracing his penis. Secondly, had he ordered the small stack of pancakes or the large rack of hostess?

The owner and madam burst in! Dave smiled and said, "Where's Moe?" Assuming he was another litigation-seeking lowlife who frequents Nevada brothels faking injury, they did little to comfort him. Of course, Dave had known coming here that there would be faking going on, but certainly not by him. Although, this brought to mind the time eight years ago when he did fake penetration.

All the while, in a backroom command center an assistant madam, Mary, was watching a replay of Dave's mishap. Laying there, he never realized the genius of the disco-ball's hidden camera that allowed Mary to cross-reference his picture with a national brothel database titled "Banned Johns." Ironically, Dave also possessed a list sharing this same name, only his was on a yellow piece of legal paper crammed next to its partner: a roll of toilet tissue in the glove compartment of his car. He referred to this list religiously while traveling and thought that one day it would be his contribution to mankind. Despite finding no system matches when she ran the industry-standard penis profile, Mary assumed Dave was scamming and now sought to determine if Beth was in cahoots.

Truly injured and receiving no sympathy from management, Dave wiggled his cell phone out of his pocket. Indifferent to whether Dave's condition was authentic or not, the owner sought to prevent bad publicity. As a veteran businessman, he calculated that the potential spike in S&M patrons would be grossly outweighed by the mainstream losses.

"You don't need to do that," he pleaded. "We can work something out. All the visits you want for a month, free!" he added.

By now Dave was on the phone, having recalled the office number of a law firm on his block.

Thinking that he was already receiving legal advice, the brothel owner quickly offered, "As many women as you want for a year!"

Had Dave been of sound mind, he surely would have accepted the first offer, regardless of the fact that the only mounting occurring was legal expense.

The lawyers' receptionist inquired, "Do you want Skatkowski Jr. or Sr.?"

"Jr.," Dave answered frantically, after briefly contemplating to whom he'd be better off conveying his situation. Thinking younger might be more liberal, he overlooked the likelihood of the father having been in either Nam or Korea.

"He's on another line. Can he call you back?"

"I'm laying on the floor of a whorehouse! Put me through right now!" Dave demanded.

"Who were you referred by?" she asked perfunctorily.

Enraged, Dave yelled, "I got the number off the bathroom wall!"

The receptionist proceeded robotically, "Did you happen to get the name of the recommender?"

"I'm in a lot of pain — could you just put me through?"

"You're where?" Skatkowski inquired.

After Dave assured the lawyer that he wasn't a high-school sophomore on lunch break, they quickly exchanged pleasantries. A gregarious-sounding fellow, Skatkowski said, "Start from the beginning."

Dave recounted, "'We should go where we're guaranteed to score,' Sam said to me after yet another frustrating night on the town. Sam was particularly bitter as he'd just been given a fake number from a phone-sex operator the night before. 'I'm not so sure I want to go to a natural food store,' I replied...."

"Where it pertains to your accident," Skatkowski interrupted.

"I'm in the room."

"What room?" he interjected.

"One of the, you know, eh, entertainment rooms. I go to sit down on a chair and next thing I know, I'm laying on my back in tremendous pain, staring at the ceiling."

"So you just slid right off the chair?" Skatkowski queried.

"I slid like a fat girl on a luge track," Dave responded, feeling somewhat petty after the comparison.

"Were you wearing pants at the time?" he posed. Not seeing the relevancy, Dave ignored the question and continued. Interrupting, Skatkowski again asked, "Did you have your pants on at the time?"

"Yes." Trying to understand the lawyer's direction and hoping there was one, Dave sought an explanation.

"Had you been *au natural*," Skatkowski said in a disturbingly relaxed tone that indicated he used this phrase routinely with clientele, "we'd be in a more precarious position. The defense would simply claim your accident to have been personally hygienically related. Now the first thing you're going to have to do is call an ambulance and get everything documented."

While Dave processed this advice, Sam sauntered in. Oblivious to any abnormality, Sam sat down on the foot of the bed. "I usually like the floor too," he said, "but here?

"I had a good time," Sam continued sheepishly, "but I might have gotten a little carried away." He proceeded to detail the debt that was sure to garnish and impoverish generations of his descendants. "Maybe management will cut me a break."

Attempting to alleviate his own suffering with

Sam's, Dave replied, "All sales are final. You can't return a sex act for a refund."

Grasping the possibility of an unstated understanding, the owner quickly said, "Let's see if you two can make it out to your car."

Another Day
at the
Orifice

Another Day at the Orifice

"I have a 10:30 appointment with Dr. Knievel," Frigitte said to the receptionist. Sitting down in her gynecologist's waiting-room, Frigitte picked up an issue of *Cosmopolitan*. Glancing at the titles, she was struck by how foreign they seemed, so removed from the articles in *Reader's Digest*. Instead of anecdotes featuring heroic golden retrievers and crime-fighting centenarians, she was now reading about buying reputable hair conditioners and hiding panty lines.

"But from whom are we hiding," Frigitte pondered, "and why would we want to hide the fact that we're wearing underwear?" In her case it was the kind of underwear that, if necessary, could carry two of every creature to safety. Even though a small thong would have clamped nicely on her slim bottom, her panties were so comprehensive they couldn't be hidden from space station view.

As Frigitte sat in the waiting-room chair, her mammoth cotton panties bunched, the wedgie causing her to sway from side to side like someone trying to kiss Ray Charles.

Dave glanced up from the training manual he was reading at his security post by the door. As he sat monitoring the waiting room, he enjoyed the relaxed accommodations the office had provided for him. His station was equipped with one of the old examination chairs. Dave was surprised as he thought they only used exam tables, but this had been custom made as the previous doctor was a midget. This doctor had entered the medical field during mid-life figuring, since he'd spent his entire existence looking at crotches, he might as well get paid for it. In medical school he had also considered becoming a proctologist, but decided that he would always need a hobby. Tragically, his wife murdered him after finding out he spent his off-days riding the escalator at Bloomingdales.

Security was a new professional situation for both Dave and the office. He sported temporary deterrents as the office struggled to quickly improvise. Dave felt a bit self-conscious having an old forceps hanging from his belt and somewhat uneasy with the canister of liquid nitrogen in his mace holder. He anxiously awaited the arrival of his back-ordered night stick, after having to use the medical equipment to pry two feuding women apart. One thing Dave did like about his post was the transparent vaginal model they'd given him to use as a pen holder.

An early blunder in which Dave mistook a middle-aged Greek man for a panty raider had ended disastrously. He'd preemptively sprayed the man who was dutifully picking up his mom, completely parting the man's eyebrows. The one arrest Dave had made certainly surprised the disruptive woman who wasn't expecting to be told to "spread 'em" while still in the waiting room.

Frigitte glanced to the far wall at the drug company brochures just beyond clear view. One titled *STD* made her think of sending a nice bouquet of flowers to friends. Another, titled *Birth Control* made her wonder, "You mean some women can't?"

For Frigitte, going to the gynecologist was like going on an archeological dig. It's some remote place down there; you probably won't find anything, but you're certain to get dirty. Called into the exam room, she began to ponder if her doctor's life was like a Nascar fan's, continually looking at the same thing and secretly hoping for an accident.

Dave had been surprised when the employment agency mentioned the job's location, but couldn't pass on the opportunity. He'd enjoyed calling a friend that evening to relate that he was filling an opening at a gynecologist's office.

On the job, Dave was stunned when he became aware of the problems these practices now faced. Following an article in a popular men's magazine on the best places to meet women, waiting-room loitering had skyrocketed.

"Any complaints?" the nurse asked as she escorted Frigitte into the examination room. "Any itching, burning during urination, unusual discharge or odor?" The nurse, having posed these same questions to Frigitte at regular checkups over the years, was overcome by a fantasy of people running out in party hats from this patient's privates, balloons floating away, crazystring shooting out and a banner reading "Grand Opening" dropping down. The nurse often wondered if even a defibrillator could bring life to this barren environment. "Any changes to your health since we last saw you? Any medical emergencies or hospitalizations?"

"Well," Frigitte said, and proceeded to recount an emergency room visit following her only attempt at sex. She'd choked on a turban while trying to give an Arab gas-station attendant head. The intern on duty theorized she would have been better off to have swallowed the entire length of turban cloth. That way she wouldn't have had to wipe for a month.

Frigitte often wondered how those turbans got so neatly wound. She envisioned certain Arabs' bathrooms equipped with a turban dispenser like a Dairy Queen soft-ice-cream machine.

Had she continued to date the Middle Easterner, it could have been ideal. She was used to being covered up and he was used to things being really dry.

Dr. Knievel had immediately, like most people, taken a liking to Dave and talked to him about the profession's deepest, darkest secrets. He spoke openly about the new trend of women getting vaginal Botox injections with the hopes of eradicating wrinkles. Unfortunately, many were left unable to retain insemination or even a tampon.

The MD even frankly admitted his own miscalculation after trying to turn his office into a boutique practice, incorporating spa amenities. He'd instituted foot reflexology as an adjunct during exams but saw no profit, since each session required two therapists. Dr. Knievel had even tried his own hand at entertainment with some quickly learned magic tricks. He soon abandoned both bits, the disappearing quarter and live dove. Also, he had decided to dismiss the Pratt Institute student hired to draw complimentary caricatures.

The doctor entered Frigitte's exam room. With the stature of an astronaut, he carried himself. Scared, apprehensive, yet curious and patriotic, he walked through the door, not knowing whether he would return and wondering how he might be remembered. His colleagues might honor his courage. They might talk about him with the likes of Lewis and Clark and Admiral Bryd, or might they ridicule him for this brazen attempt? These thoughts gave way to a blissful inner silence.

Shortly into the examination, though, he began to panic. Had he underestimated frigidity — his foe? Was he already within the deadly grip of hypothermia? Reassuring himself of his cognitive state, he pondered whether to continue or turn back.

Commandingly he said, "Nurse, give me my ski mask." Then, with a detectable shake to his voice, "Goggles!" Now moving forward, committing completely, he passed the point of no return. The terrain was formidable, yet he knew weather was his true enemy. Soon exhausted, he dreamt of ramen soup. Checking his barometer, he noted a change in atmospheric pressure. There seemed to be some funk moving in from the south.

He remembered being in medical school, brimming with confidence and devoid of fear, scoffing at a senior faculty member's comment, "He who lives by the forceps, dies by…." However, he was reassured by his ingenuity as he had been careful to leave bread crumbs along the way, solidifying that he would be able to retrace his steps. Overwhelmed by the sight of Frigitte's vast unexplored territory, he unwaveringly planted the American flag.

Entering a delusional fantasy brought on by immense feelings of success, the doctor pictured himself as he stepped to the podium to receive his lifetime Golden Stirrups award. He envisioned his name as the guest of honor, embossed on the awards-ceremony invitation above the date, location, and a line that read, "B.Y.O. OB/GYN."

"I present the man, the myth, the adventurer — Dr. Beaver Knievel!" the MC introduced.

Knievel triumphantly opened his speech, "Because it was there!" As he stepped from the stage, he was mobbed by fledgling gynecologists still green from their first exams. He enthusiastically, with the remaining fingers that weren't lost to frostbite, signed their note pads.

Alert again, the doctor proceeded to extricate himself from the exam. All the while, Frigitte had been pondering why she'd never seen KY jelly on the health food store shelves and whether it would be good with almond butter.

Back at his desk, Dr. Knievel proclaimed to her as he smiled, "Everything's fine!"

"Doctor," the nurse said, "What do you want for lunch?"

He thought for a moment, and then replied, "Soup sounds good."

No
Artificial
Flavors
or
Insemination

No Artificial Flavors or Insemination

Times were tough for Dave. His ever-so-modest checking account was shrinking faster than Dr. Ruth or the johnson of an unsuspecting gala attendee on whom she'd chosen to demonstrate her latest lap-dance video, "Last Chance Lap Dance." The only wood present would be the mahogany on the shoulders of pallbearers for the men subjected to watching it. However, Dr. Ruth's previous release was a smashing success, "Horny Old Women and the Men Incapable of Saying 'Leave Me Alone!'" Dave waited for an opportunity to make a few dollars like Dr. Ruth did for her spot in the "Got Milk" ad campaign.

At his age, Dave no longer felt comfortable asking his folks for assistance. "You know, you're not eighteen anymore," he'd said to himself. Jobless and without any leads promising, Dave still wasn't as desperate and pathetic as the celebrity wannabees who backstab their peers and perform sexual favors on the exotic pets of studio execs. All this, done for airtime where they're eating elephant testicles and drinking coffee filtered through the hairnet of a lunch lady at a Greek elementary school.

Dave needed money to stay off the street. It was the last day of October and his rent was due. "How good a hobo would a hypochondriac make?" he asked himself.

Skimming his brain again for any possibilities, Dave remembered seeing an ad for a fertility clinic offering $200 for eligible sperm donors. However, having certain reservations, he'd dismissed the idea. How could he be all right knowing he had a child somewhere? But now, traumatized by the thought of soup kitchen sanitation, he concluded that maybe it was actually a noble act to give those not capable the gift of life. Confident this was the right decision, Dave dressed as if he were going to the gym. He thought it would be the most appropriate attire, since for some men this was their only form of exercise. He splashed on cologne, then regretted it, wondering if the receptionist might think it was a ritual.

As he walked toward the clinic, he began to feel self-conscious. Would anyone there recognize him? Who might he bump into: a neighbor, his high-school driver education teacher, his future father-in-law?

What would his girlfriend say? Dave envisioned how the conversation might go. She'd say, "How could you do something weird like that?" And he'd calmly reply, "Don't worry, I'll make more." But what if he didn't? What if this was the end of his allotted production, the last of a limited series? It could end as quickly as Kathy Lee's clothing line when the traveling carnival hit that tiny Guatemalan village.

Dave had decided to walk, as he couldn't sacrifice round-trip cab fare from his future earnings. However, he thought it would be amusing to know he was passing a cab driver fertility-clinic money. Rethinking the oddity of this, he realized cabbies, for sure, had picked up fares outside peep shows or possibly even chauffeured Pee Wee Herman.

As the blocks faded behind him Dave wondered, "Did he have the walk of a man destined for sperm donation? Were his intentions clear for all to see, blatantly displayed in his physiologically altered gait? On his return, might people glance at him like he was a creep; would he feel as if he were wearing a trenchcoat and knee-high black socks?

Might groups of teenagers yell slurs like spunkman and jizz monger, all the while making obscene hand gestures alluding to what he'd just done?"

Admitting to himself, "On the road to nowhere, I'm in the passing lane," Dave pushed on the door. Nothing. He glanced up at the decal — "Pull." Entering, he paused mid-stroke. Expecting the waiting room to be empty, he was stunned as it resembled a sorority yard sale in Tokyo where all used panties were only twenty-one yen. He heard in his mind a frustrated customer saying, "Oh no, not for barbecue — tong!"

Dave, green to fertility clinics, had stumbled in on Halloween, the only day for anonymity and, therefore, their busiest day of the year. Not in costume and mistaken for an employee, he nearly dropped the specimen jar an old guy handed him.

Chaos abounded in the small waiting room that held double its intended capacity. To his left sat a man dressed as Elvis, looking at a *Playboy.* To his right, Edward Scissorhands and Gandhi were wrestling back and forth in an ominously escalating tug-of-war over a particularly enticing Victoria's Secret catalog. Gandhi pulled unwaveringly, despite not having wrapped his garment for sufficient athletic support.

"My elbow!" he yelled, as he grabbed his now-limp donation arm. Frantically, he rewrapped his kadhi shawl tightly around his arm to avoid the rerouting of bloodflow, hoping to prevent swelling in the wrong place.

Realizing the potential liability in an attempt at donation by either Gandhi or Edward Scissorhands, the nurse summoned Elvis.

Meanwhile, The King had become overly aroused from perusing the *Playboys*. Elvis, now looking like a hounddog, sheepishly headed for the door.

Returning to her chart, the nurse checked the box labeled "Premature Donation" and proceeded to the next name.

Dave moved forward with great trepidation, like Anna Nicole Smith scouting a nursing home and hoping it wasn't a Medicaid facility. He commented to the receptionist, "That guy's Gary Coleman costume is amazing. It's so life-like!"

"That is Gary Coleman," the not-so-festive receptionist replied.

Dave thought to himself, "I guess that gives a new meaning to the expression 'being hard up for work.' "

Following the Coleman blunder, he thought better of complimenting the receptionist on the believability of her Rosie O'Donnell costume. She forcefully handed him a clipboard holding a lengthy form. Dave, expecting the staff to more closely resemble that of Hooters, couldn't help wonder how greatly the receptionist, who reminded him of his high-school gym teacher, hurt business. Fourth-quarter profits were certainly going to be down.

Dave sat down on a very stylish and modern sofa. The coffee table in front of him sported a number of Larry Flynt publications, a *Sports Illustrated* swimsuit issue, some *Playboys* and an issue of *Field and Stream.* After completing the initial generic-info page of the questionnaire, he flipped to page two and things got much more personal. Page two's heading read, "Eligibility Requirements." Below he read a list of items that would disqualify a potential donor. The stipulations included anyone who's read *Chicken Soup for the Erectile Dysfunctional* or *Who Moved My Penis?,* the memoir of John Wayne Bobbit.

Beneath this was an area asking for detailed descriptions of any accidents or mishaps which may have caused damage to the groin region. Dave wrote, "Not applicable," although he'd always remember clearly the time he was playing cowboys and Indians with his brother. In an act that, if done by a contemplative adult would have made "Jackass: The Movie," Dave, as the cowboy, leapt from the deck onto his makeshift horse-in-waiting, a bike tied to a tree. The posse would not ride that day.

Walking past and noticing the stress-filled look on Dave's face, a nurse dressed as an angel said, "Don't worry! Here, nobody gets voted out of the waiting room."

Beginning to tire, Dave resorted to cheating on the page where you're to identify the words that don't agree. Getting help from a friend via cell phone, he was able to preserve energy for the essay. Completing stage one of the application process and feeling he'd proven himself quite the intellect, Dave was set to move on.

Deciding, instead, on a short break, Dave talked extensively with a Jerry Lewis impersonator. Not only did he learn where all the kids came from, but also that there were three classification levels of donors. This being his maiden fertility-clinic trip, it came as a surprise that all donations were not compensated for equally. Pay directly corresponded to the level at which donors were assessed. Level 1 donations, known on the street as Angel Juice, were the most-highly coveted, thought to possess all the qualities of the universally desired Renaissance man.

Mr. Lewis' gabby impersonator volunteered the pride he had for his actions now being open and legitimate, having left behind the underworld of blackmarket fertility trade. Gone were the days of back-alley donations, where instead of being handed paperwork by a woman in a lab coat, he had been assisted by a woman in a fake-fur coat. Unregulated, he gallantly recalled the days he'd completed three or four donations, sometimes while holding a beer in one hand. Dave wondered if he should save his grandmother a telethon telephone call and give this guy the money to walk out the door.

Level 2, which categorized most donors, was the essential material for a quality human being and was the level at which Jerry speculated Dave would be assessed. Level 3, he revealed, was available strictly for those with a limited budget and special needs, such as having to become pregnant quickly to coerce their way into a dying tycoon's will and not having the credit to finance. Or possibly someone might want a Christmas gift for the sister they hated. Dave would never plunge his hand into a stocking carefree again.

As Dave once again contemplated his decision

to part with his DNA, he reminded himself of the date, October 31, and the need to pay the rent. “Should I have just gone on Ebay?” he wondered.

Walking down the hall to the physical testing room, panic overtook him. How could he compete with the doping practices employed by other donors. During one of his many waiting-room conversations, he'd stumbled into the world of performance-enhanced donating. To get to that Level 1 ranking and larger paycheck, donors allegedly went to great lengths. He'd heard tales of some not wearing pants for a week before, receiving take-out food from behind their apartment doors, and others making pilgrimages to Chinatown pharmacies to acquire rare, foreign roots and animal excrement potions. One avid tofu eater even claimed to have gone cold turkey. Some practices described were so bizarre they probably would never have been considered by the International Olympic Committee. With the fertility industry's apocalypse pending due to the cloning revolution, the rush for donor compensation had reached an all-time frenzy.

One waiting-room regular had even polluted Dave's mind with a barrage of donor-related urban legends. There was The Bastard Offspring Murderer who, after reaching adulthood, would retrieve the money donors had made prior to offing them. Also, the Unixer, a woman who roams the city castrating hotdog vendors. Some in-the-know argue, however, that her donor father was technically a knish seller.

Leaving the garbed crowd in the waiting room, Dave made a mental note to forgo future Halloween costume rentals as he headed for the physical testing room. He was met by a college-aged fellow sporting the look of a man who'd wished he'd applied himself in high school. Expecting a rather strenuous evaluation of both strength and endurance, Dave was surprised to simply be asked to simultaneously pat the top of his head with one hand and air-masturbate with the other.

Then Dave was presented with an element of surprise. The tester asked, "If you could inseminate one woman throughout history, alive or dead, who would it be and why?" Pausing in disgust at the suggestion of deceased insemination, Dave was relieved when the young man continued, "You know, if you could go back in time."

Without further hesitation Dave responded, "Ethel Merman," but was frightened because he didn't know why. Stressed and fatigued from the mental drain the experience had taken on him, Dave felt he could skip the donation room and go straight to the nap room.

On his way back to the waiting room, Dave's mind filled with guilt. He thought, "I'm having a child I'll never get to meet. What kind of father does this make me, profiting off of my parental negligence? It's not right! I can't do it!" Problem was, he already had.

Back in the waiting room which was now filled with prospective buyers, Dave realized he had to take corrective measures. Many of the ladies, some in Halloween attire, eyed him like the piece of meat he felt he'd just betrayed. Frantic to get back to the front desk he found himself standing behind twelve women who may or may not have been a WNBA team. Like a Japanese man who had over-indulged at a Mexican restaurant, he excused himself profusely as he cut to the head of the line. There Dave encountered a buyer dressed as Joan of Arc, leaning on the counter, chatting amicably with the receptionist. "Pardon me, but I have a little problem," he interrupted.

Begrudgingly the receptionist responded, "We got Viagra, but it'll be deducted from your pay."

"No, actually I've already donated," Dave said. The Rosie look-alike and Joan stared at him perplexedly. Knowing he'd receive about as much sympathy as Howard Stern, he blurted, "I need my donation back." Now beaming with self-righteousness, Dave embodied the physiology of a donor's modern-day Rosa Parks. "My donation, I want it back!" he demanded.

"What is this, some kind of bit?" the receptionist asked.

Dave, now a Paxil poster-child, was so stressed and anxious that his mind heard, "Do you want a bit?" "I want the whole thing," he insisted.

"Look mister, you're gonna have to leave."

"Maybe you think I'm some kind of weirdo." Then he thought, "Who wouldn't?" Stabilizing, Dave continued, "Let me simply have my specimen and I'll give you the money back."

"Oh, I get it, you go around looking for kicks by getting-off in different clinics. This is the last time I'm going to ask you to leave!"

"Please, let me explain myself," Dave countered. "I just feel uncomfortable fathering a child this way."

"So you're saying you got some kinda separation anxiety or something?" Rosie asked.

"I think he's one of those hoarders," Joan said. "You know, the kind that has a yard sale but won't sell anything."

"It's not a mental problem; it's a personal issue," Dave contended.

"All right, a Level 2 purchase — that'll be four hundred dollars."

"Four hundred dollars!" Dave exclaimed. "But you just paid me two!" He didn't know what her sense was, but it clearly wasn't humor or common.

"That's right! A Level 2 donation pays two hundred dollars. A Level 2 specimen sells for four hundred dollars."

Overwhelmed, Dave questioned, "That can't be right?"

"Do you have our discount card?" the receptionist asked. Dave, stunned at the unfolding situation, was unable to reply. The receptionist continued, "If you have our card, it'll only be three hundred dollars."

Dave solemnly muttered, "No."

With the learned behavior of a chimpanzee who's been trained to give colonics so the nurse can fill out reality-show applications, she recited, "For only ten dollars you can get the card today."

"I'm not a consumer; I just don't want to be a part of this process. How can it be four hundred dollars?" he continued.

"Look, we run a business here not some adult funhouse. We have overhead and processing."

"All you did was carry my vial in from the other room."

"Either I need four hundred dollars or I'm going to help the next person in line."

Completely desperate, Dave asked, "Four hundred, are you sure?"

"One Level 2 specimen, four hundred. If you want to buy more, we can work with you."

Unable to withstand getting sidetracked, he pondered why anyone would buy in bulk. Was he unaware of some new fad where groups of ladies had fertility parties and sat around eating humus and inseminating one another?

She continued, "The only other card we honor is AARP."

Realizing he'd have to exit and regroup, Dave asked, "Could you then just set it aside for me?"

Joan, looking Dave up and down while adjusting her pants and further confusing him as to whether she was a donor, a buyer or both, said, "I don't think you have to worry about it."

The receptionist followed, "I'll need a fifty-percent deposit to set it aside — you know, to prevent window shopping."

Dave walked out the door a much older man. Was this some type of cosmic reaction to his questionable behavior? Hitting the sidewalk, he was confronted by an angry group of picketers. Glancing around he immediately assessed them as professionals. These people had causes, too many causes, some of which directly conflicted with one another. Last week they were saving the seals, while next week they would be trying to boost the Eskimo economy. Often the protesters found themselves on-site, picketing each others' interests. These were people who sported erasable signs, with a cloth and magic marker, so they could spontaneously begin a new campaign. Perceptibly uninformed about the issues, they marched and yelled, sometimes mismatched to the location. As Dave walked away, he heard one woman who thought she was at a nurses' rights rally yell, "No bedpan hands!"

Fearing the possibility of anonymous fatherhood, Dave figured he might raise the other two hundred by convincing someone he knew to donate. He racked his brain on the way home; who could he get? Arriving quickly at the realization that he didn't know too many people he could ask to donate sperm on his behalf, he considered scouting his high-school yearbook which he knew would be a gold mine. He directly recalled many troubled classmates showing him the donor-clinic location in pamphlets which contained detailed map drawings from the local go-kart track and Planned Parenthood, where they had dropped their impregnated girlfriend-of-the-week. The guidance counselor had given them these brochures entitled *Make Donation Your Vocation,* figuring they might as well earn legitimate income from their propensity for fathering illegitimate kids.

The practicality of recruiting these former classmates waned, however, as Dave surmised they would probably be hundred dollar, Level 3 classification donations. This would be useful only if Dave could find the Rickett brothers and get them both to donate. That scenario seemed highly complex. Besides, he thought, chances are good one of them has already donated today.

Dave then thought of a college student he'd mentored who had slipped into phone-sex addiction, becoming so psychologically conditioned that he wanked at the ring of a phone. Though this promising protégé had slipped into a bizarre and socially debilitating condition, Dave knew he'd be perfect but didn't know how often he checked his email.

Deciding instead to call an old roommate who frequently donated because he always wanted to "give a little back," Dave talked rapidly, getting right to the point. "Bill, could you do me a huge favor and go down to the fertility clinic and make a donation for me?"

His friend, amused and inspired, "You mean like a gift to the United Way and say I'm donating on your behalf?" Now fully rolling with it, "Or if you'd rather, maybe I could use a Unicef container and send it in with your name on it?" Laughing profusely, Bill finally offered, "Sure I can do it and still have time for a nap before wrestling comes on."

Dave, relieved and filled with appreciation, "Look at it like this — not only are you doing me a favor, you're doing yourself a favor. Seriously buddy, I owe you one."

Bill walked into the waiting room after completing his donation. He and Dave embraced, uniting like separated Siamese twins. Luckily however, they didn't share a scrotum or the situation would still be unresolved. Dave was quick to separate from the embrace, as it was drawing stares.

"I'm glad to help out a friend. I mean it's a hell of a lot better then helping you move."

"Let me just make the buyback and we'll be out of here," Dave said.

Back at the counter, the receptionist's imposing figure gazed at him, "Can I help you?"

"Ah, yes," Dave replied, "I was in earlier."

"Yeah, I remember you," the Rosie look-alike said.

"I would like to purchase my donation which you set aside," Dave replied.

Glancing at Bill who was standing a few feet away, she said, "You know this isn't an adoption agency. One of you has to be a female." As she laughed, her monstrous muscles jiggled but her Popeyesque forearm didn't. Her cupped hand, a form of job-related carpal tunnel, gripped an empty donation vial. "Here it is!"

Dave, thoroughly incensed, but not to the point of contacting the Better Business Bureau, demanded as he slapped the additional two hundred dollars on the counter, "Just get it!"

Looking around, she said, "Your donation must have already been transferred to our sales department. Go down the hall, second door on the right."

As Dave headed for the sales department, he worried whether having checked the donor box on the back of his driver's license meant EMS would give him a handjob instead of defibrillation.

When he knocked on the open door of the office, his senses were overloaded by its contents. A man, so hairy that Dave was confused as to which way he was facing, sat at a desk. The air smelled like a fusion of Tabasco and over-tanned flesh.

Jumping to his feet, the man said, "Come on in, I'm Dwayne. Let me show you some brochures of what your kid might look like if you decide to go with a Level 1 purchase."

Envisioning the stuffed remains of deceased donors displayed on the walls and still a bit fearful of being enslaved on a donor chain gang, Dave cautiously replied, "I already know what I want."

Before he could continue, Dwayne shook his hand, "I admire a man who's decisive."

"Actually, I donated this morning and I would like to buy it back," explained Dave. "Here's the tracking number."

"Ah...OK, you are aware sir, this is only a Level 2?"

"Yeah...."

Interrupting Dave, Dwayne continued, "For only the additional cost of a microwave we could have you walking outa here with a Level 1."

Thinking the man was confused, Dave clarified, "I just want to purchase my own donation."

"But why not consider a 1? We've got some great sales specials this week including the third cousin of Michael Jordan," he offered.

"What do you think I'm going to do with it?" Dave regretted posing the question, realizing most buyers weren't in his shoes.

Readjusting, Dwayne pitched, "I have something called the Frat Pack. It's a dozen, really-quality Level 3's."

Now more relaxed, Dave explained, "I just want to buy my donation and dispose of it."

Smiling Dwayne said, "Dave, you know I was a lot like you once, just trying to make ends meet. After years of donating, I decided to start my own business. With only three Frederick's of Hollywood catalogs and a shoe box, I struggled to make ends meet. Then one day at a bus stop in Moline, I was inspired to create this clinic. An old man approached me and said, 'If you build it, they will come.' Today, I'm expanding my empire with drive-thru donation centers."

Dave slapped his claim stub on the desk and

demanded the container. Reluctantly, Dwayne retrieved the vial from the freezer. He handed it over, wrapped in a bumper sticker carrying the clinic's name and reading, "I'd Rather Be Donating!"

As Dave strode through the waiting room toward the front door, he saw a man in a suit and mask dressed as Martin Luther King. Dr. King was slouched in the same chair that had been occupied by the other King. Pushing on the door to exit, Dave noticed that the man was snoring heavily and couldn't help thinking, "I hope he doesn't have a wet dream."

Best
in
Chow

Best in Chow

"You could have gotten the same ideas at Home Depot," a mid-western retired homemaker said. Bored and frustrated, she stood atop The Great Wall of China shaking her head. Meanwhile, her husband examined the structure intently.

Indifferent to her fatigue he said, "I'm thinkin' of startin' it behind the shed and runnin' it clear cross the septic field." Bob had decided, in order to keep his neighbor's dog from defecating on his lawn, to build a wall in his and Doris' backyard.

A year ago, with his architectural vision unclear, he conceded to needing conceptual assistance. It was then he booked the trip to China. Bob, however, was not alone in his search for inspiration, as hundreds of other men just like him explored The Wall. Viewed by satellite, they dotted its walkway like cellulite on a pantyline. Studying The Wall's four-thousand-mile expanse, most were somewhere in the middle looking for an end, all simultaneously measuring, feeling and speculating. Impossible to impress, Bob stood there talking on his cell phone with his grandson, saying, "The Wall is pretty good."

Doris' only consolation with this trip's destination was that she knew she wouldn't have to get directions after Bob got lost. They watched as a suicidal obsessive-compulsive circled one location after another on The Wall, unable to decide which spot had exactly the right Feng Shui for jumping.

"Construction began on The Great Wall in 214 B.C.," Dave announced to a group of senior citizens from New Orleans. Wanting to experience more of the world, he had taken a position advertised in AARP as a travel guide for The Lost Continence Tours.

Fed up with the job, Dave now planned to finance his world exploration through other means as he'd tolerated enough from these rowdy seniors. After imbibing recklessly in a Calcutta stripbar, one drunk geezer had crudely blurted, "Loose the dot!"

Another man had vehemently argued his theories of the Kama Sutra with Dave. "If Gandhi had gotten an erection he would have tipped over," the man had contended. "Ninety percent of the Kama Sutra is impossible!"

Following these incidents in India, Dave had even considered becoming a snake charmer but didn't know if he could make it past the learning curve. Besides, in the high-school band the only instrument he had learned to play was the tuba.

Entry posts of The Great Wall were still manned to facilitate vehicles passing through. Personnel gazed in all directions, ready to process incoming conveyances.

Atop The Wall another retired couple passed, the man stopping every twenty feet to take a picture. Bob wondered if the man was intending to make his own puzzle or was too cheap to buy the disposable panoramic. The view out over the Asian continent was magnificent. Bob saw two unfortunate teenagers dusting themselves off after an ill-fated attempt to pop a wheelie on a 1950's two-seater bike. He and Doris paused, basking in the afternoon sun over one of the entrances as several employees escorted a fruit truck through. Doris envisioned her overly ambitious spouse realizing he'd built his wall to include some of their neighbor's property and having to knock it down.

An out-of-place octogenarian from Dave's tour strolled along the top of The Wall with Mardi Gras beads swinging from his walker. He yelled down to a Chinese woman performing slow, stylized movements near the base, “What are you doing?”

Looking up, she called back, “Tai Chi.”

Interpreting this as “tight jeans,” the man assumed she was flirting with him and shouted, “Show me your tits!” Ten minutes later, with the woman having only raised her shirt to her belly button, the dejected geriatric walked away in disappointment.

It was at this point that Bob saw something in the distance. At first he thought it to be the sun’s reflection off a nomad’s hat. Doris noticed Bob’s fixation and quickly adjusted her gaze. In an attempt to get a better look, they made their way to the nearest pay telescope. After inserting quarters in the telescope just the way they’d done on top of the Empire State Building, the two were confused as the viewfinder only opened half way. Anxious to get a better look, they sacrificed new quarters in a different telescope, but had the same result. Perplexed, Bob squinted to take in the sight. Bumbling, he stammered, “Looks like a giant sausage.”

Doris fumbled through her purse to find the printout that accompanied Bob’s latest prescription. As she read frantically through the pages of bizarre possible side effects, she found nothing about pressed-meat hallucinations. The only mention of anything even remotely close was the possible inability to taste Spam.

Bob's attention was no longer on the distant object but next to him, where two men he recognized as Larry David and Jerry Seinfeld strolled past. He overheard, "What's the deal with this wall? It just goes straight. I mean, how can you build a wall around nothing?" Eavesdropping on the pair, Bob heard them contemplating plans for a Seinfeld sitcom return. They envisioned the gang living in Beijing and operating an American restaurant where they subjected randomly selected patrons to absurd wait times.

Doris, looking toward the countryside, commented, "What is that? It looks like a bratwurst."

As this object moved slowly closer, those on The Wall called out different types of link meat. Then all fell silent as the object mounted a small knoll about a hundred yards from The Wall. It was a thirty-foot-long dachshund. Most were speechless as this mammoth, phallic pooch advanced. A lesbian, leaning forcefully against The Wall, gripped her partner's hand tighter as they shared expressions of jealousy and curiosity.

Exalted Chinese shouted expressions of joy as the apparent, colossal canine reached The Wall.

Legend had predicted that in the 21st century, in a Year of the Dog, salvation to prevent famine would arrive. It would be bestowed as a creature so large as to bring bounty and celebration to all the land. Lore had it this would continue to occur yearly, corresponding directly to the animal calendar. As word of the arrival of the dog spread faster than the new disease they might contract from eating it, townsfolk started planning side dishes for the next calendar-year's pig.

The lesbian couple watched intently as the dog surged for the gate. It pressed right through the huge, unopened screendoor. Part way through the dachshund stopped, its girth preventing a smooth entry. It backed out slightly, then lunged again, this time continuing on to the other side.

Inside the hollow dachshund, Joan steered the Trojan Dog with one hand and browsed the latest catalog from Lands End with the other. She was accompanied by several other disenchanted, ex-PETA members. They had formed their own alliance, as they felt PETA's dogma had become too mainstream.

"I knew I shouldn't have eaten all that tofu before getting in here with no bathroom," said Dan.

"I thought for sure you'd just sweat it out,"

replied his girlfriend, Frita, who was now attempting to avert disaster by performing emergency reflexology on Dan. With dangerously restricted ventilation and poor air circulation, the cabin smelled worse then a real dog's colon.

As these vigilante vegans neared the village, their fears intensified. "They must know it's not a real dog. They can see it's not licking itself," Sarah uttered after regaining consciousness from hyperventilating during a relaxation breathing exercise. As they pressed on, the gang's energy was sustained by soy bars and their drive to expose the cruelty involved with many countries' culinary practices.

Behind the dachshund, Bob, Doris and the rest of the tourists who'd been on top of The Wall joined the parade to the nearest village. Ten miles away, a chauffeur, high on methamphetamines, ran frantically towards the village, pulling a rickshaw with his teeth for his dominatrix rider. On board was Double Porked Cook, a celebrity Chinese chef and porn star who had been summoned to prepare the dog. Her provincial cable show pulled in high ratings as she chopped and screwed her way into people's kitchens and dining rooms. Her show called "Eat Me" fused sex with food and even sported a dash of comedy. Her comedy was raw like the meat she handled. "It's not the size of your wok, but what you do with it," was how she opened every show. Fortunately, she avoided dishes that required basting.

As details of the legend spread, Bob said to Doris, "Isn't this great! We always said we wanted to try the native dishes when we traveled." In his mind he imagined a friendly local giving Doris the recipe. He envisioned cosmic justice as he fired up his barbecue wearing an apron that read, "Pooped on My Lawn for the Last Time!" "This would be even better than building that wall," he thought to himself regarding remedying the neighbor's colonically challenged dog.

"We're almost there!" Joan announced to the cabin. This notification caused some panic as the crew hurriedly prepared to disembark. From the uneven terrain everyone's sandals had slid to the rear wall and now nobody knew whose Tevas were whose.

After finally getting organized, the crew returned to their conversation about earth-friendly products. What had begun as a friendly exchange had escalated into a heated competition with each vying to be the most diligent practitioner. The claims elevated until all fell silent after Frita blurted, "Well, Dan and I use condoms that are guaranteed not tested on animals!" Contraception was a sore spot for Sarah, as she juggled eight kids due to her conundrum of both eschewing lambskin and being latex sensitive.

The enormous dachshund made its way through the outskirts of the village. It proceeded to the provincial capitol building, one of China's rare, new domed structures that resembled a giant fire hydrant. Thousands of cheering onlookers halted their celebration as the dog, with the capitol building to its starboard side, raised its leg. Horror filled the people's eyes as they anticipated a catastrophic flood. With its leg held at full spread revealing the dog's uncastrated glory, all could see a portal open at the tip of the penis. Faces changed from fear to confusion as instead of a mighty gush of urine, slid a group of people who, gauging from their appearance, may have been soaked in urine.

While some onlookers dropped their jaws and their chop sticks, Double Porked Cook stood her ground at the head of her rickshaw caravan, eating one of her signature take-out dishes, "Cup O' Poodles." Behind her were three additional rickshaws filled with her exclusive line of international canine sauces, including her famous "Yorkshire Terriaki."

The foreigners chanted animal rights mantras

as they exited, some slogans discernible, others a bit obscure.

Bob said to Doris, "They must be those PETA people. The initials stand for something."

Pondering this wonderful organization that had brought such a magnanimous gift, but not understanding their chants, the Chinese struggled to unravel the puzzle. Following a grand epiphany, one of the villagers shouted, "I've heard of this group — it stands for People for the Edible Treatment of Animals."

Now Joan was face to face with the famous chef. "How can you eat dog?" she demanded.

"I have as many ways as there are breeds at the Westminster Kennel Club," the chef replied brazenly. Defiantly, she continued, "Had that Spuds MacKenzie been over here, I would have made beer stew out of him."

With the impressive equipment the dog was packing, Double Porked Cook contemplated sparing it to use on her upcoming sweeps special entitled "Doggie Style." Then the chef in a friendlier tone said, "Look, we just want to eat."

Joan, a bit disarmed by the more personal exchange, questioned, "But why do you have to eat dog?"

Double Porked Cook leaned in and dignifiedly replied, "Confucius once said, 'He who eat whole dog, have no sad tail.'"

The Ghost of Pornos Past

The Ghost of Pornos Past

Dave found himself inadvertently transforming into a talented playboy. Although not genetically blessed with the tongue of Gene Simmons or the lower half of Wilt Chamberlain, the women still swooned. Dave fortunately possessed a perfectly paced, palsyic left hand, that during a seizure was said by the ladies to be nirvana. His well-trained aid dog, Pavlov, would bring him a rubber and a poncho when he detected an onset.

This irresistible, physical idiosyncrasy enabled Dave to work the field like a pregnant Asian woman in the rice patties. And he can now safely say that rice is edible, that the Hippie tales of women squatting in the fields, giving birth and immediately resuming work were erroneous. Turns out, his fears of spooning brown rice with placenta were completely irrational.

At the time, Dave was dating a beautifully

uninhibited nurse, Maria. Thinking there was nothing new left for him to experience, he unwaveringly debated the most rigorous skeptics. They'd ask, "What about female orgasmic urinary incontinence?"

Dave, with biceps worthy of professional wrestling attention, replied, "Developed these muscles flipping my mattress."

Soon, though, he began to hear things in the brief interims of silence when not deafened by the sound of his own penis cranking to attention. There were other supernatural noises in the room, sounds similar to that of grinding mechanical devices battling gravity, like that of the Rockefeller Center Christmas tree being winched into position. Laying in bed, Dave began to hear, not chains being dragged or shutters slamming, but the squeaking of a bed in manic use. Perfectly still, he listened as accompanying this were moans and heavy breathing. At first Dave simply laughed and thought, "It must just be Maria's stomach growling." But as the racket persisted, he became increasingly perplexed. It wasn't her stomach; it was clearly coming from below her navel.

As the nights passed, the noises got louder and strange occurrences started happening around the house. The lights turned on and off, and the stereo unpredictably began to play. Most puzzling of all was that it continually piped out Barry White. Dave searched endlessly for a logical explanation to these peculiar events. To calm his mind, he had to find some plausible reason for the occurrences. He thought, "Could the electronic tag still attached to Maria's newly purchased panties be triggering our electrical system?"

The bizarre goings-on surrounding Maria continued. By the next morning, Dave's dog, Pavlov, was mysteriously crazed. Running around the house severely agitated, he desperately dry-humped thin air. At first it appeared that not only was he trying to catch his own tail but also screw it. From one room to another he went, even thrusting while airborne, as he charged through the house. As in a perverse ballet routine, he pirouetted around the apartment, unsynchronized with his partner.

Had Pavlov's castration left him with great insecurities about his manhood? Did he now feel his remaining potential would merely be suited for a flying insect? What was taking place under this roof? Were Maria and Pavlov stricken by the same affliction or was this purely coincidental?

Unsure where to turn for guidance, Dave recalled insightful advice from a pet psychic,

Cynthia, who had channeled his eternally beloved, deceased dog, Pinãta. Pinãta, however, was still with Dave in body and in spirit. Financially strapped and unable to meet the monetary demands of the regional cryogenics lab, Dave had his beloved buddy suspended in his freezer, tucked lovingly between a Hungry Man meatloaf dinner and his girlfriend's Weight Watcher turkey.

Following those psychic sessions, Dave regularly, in Pinãta's memory, walked the streets of their neighborhood with an empty, small plastic bag on his hand. Maria was still adjusting to waking with Dave's cold, wet nose in her ass.

Knowing he needed to move quickly concerning the current mysterious phenomena, Dave put his monetary concerns aside and made an appointment with Cynthia for the next day. He remembered at the end of their last session being stunned at her bill. "Four hundred dollars for an hour?" he had exclaimed. "Besides, you slept half the time."

Claiming to be on canine time, Cynthia had calmly explained that Dave had actually gotten her entire work day, as an hour to her was really seven.

Completely engulfed in sentimentality, Dave

reminisced like a flasher now residing at an assisted-living nudist colony. He recalled the psychic session where they had discovered that the Great Beyond was, indeed, filled with meadows of bacon and obese women in super-tight spandex, attempting to run.

Luckily though, some things remained unknown. Like whether it was Pinãta or his old high-school friend who was responsible for the funny smell the lady across the hall complains her doormat now has. Also, Maria had wanted to know if Dave had ever taken her custom-made, oversized diaphragm to the park. She feared he'd used it as a frisbee to play catch with Pinãta, knowing his aspirations of their being on ESPN.

Smiling, Dave recalled how later that evening he had followed Cynthia's lead and tried to explain to Maria that he, too, was now running on canine time. That the lovemaking session she'd experienced as three minutes was actually twenty-one.

As they dressed in the morning to leave, things only became stranger. The water kettle that was boiling began to whistle, but now it resembled the whistle sent by a construction worker to a leggy passerby. Beginning to get spooked, Maria asked Dave to drive her to work. Reaching the garage, they both froze as the car not only was running, but the engine kept revving like a Driver Ed student was behind the wheel for the first time. Furthermore, not having been driven at night in days, what were the headlights doing on? Had it not been for Maria's experiencing these things concurrently, Dave might have chalked it up to brain damage incurred during his queening phase. Looking back, it amused him that to use his face as a bicycle seat, he'd engaged a woman who was so morbidly obese she couldn't ride one.

Nearing the hospital where Maria worked, they sat silently at a stoplight. Suddenly a giant crate outside a fruit market gave way. They stared as melons careened out, bouncing and rolling on the sidewalk. Parking at the hospital, it was apparent that Maria was feeling something. She began touching herself and even to the layman, although she was a trained medical professional, it clearly wasn't any type of examination.

"I'm so horny!" she moaned.

Dave wondered what was going on, as this wasn't in accordance with their every-fifth-day schedule. Had she switched to the swingers' calendar and not told him? Writhing, she reached for Dave's groin. Still writhing she reached again, like a little person going for a box of Wheaties on the top shelf. She undid her seatbelt, reached up under her skirt and slid her pantyhose down to her knees. Violently she spread her legs; they snapped back together with force so great as to send undulations up her body. Dave never would have guessed that her intense fear of runners and her propensity to wear a new pair every day could have dire consequences.

As crazed sexually as she now was, Dave's concerns drifted to the fact that he'd just gotten the car detailed last week. He closed his eyes as Maria removed his unit. Then, in what he guessed was an amazingly acrobatic move, she lunged toward him. As she began grinding, Dave listened to what sounded like gears. "Heads up!" she yelled.

He peered over to see Maria thrusting upon the bobble-head Chihuahua he had suctioned on his dashboard. "Oh Maria!" Dave replied, wondering how he would move her to his much-smaller, less-versatile apparatus. Seeing that she was too bothered to bother, he watched in awe as she cranked away. Sweating, she tore open her shirt. Running her hands through her hair, Maria screamed. She dismounted, looking like someone who'd just done an imaginary cross-country trip on a mechanical bull, now tired and out of quarters.

As she headed to work, Dave sat alone in dismay. While he returned his johnson to its rightful place, he was surprised that the interior of the car was unscathed. He'd expected the inside of his windows to look like the car had been crammed with a dozen clowns from the nudist-colony circus.

The day transpired tediously as Dave contemplated what could possibly be going on at the hospital. His concerns paled in comparison to the events that unfolded. The raging sex drive which had manifested in the car that morning continued to intensify. Frenzied and out of control, Maria masturbated in a coma patient's room. Her moaning and panting were so intense the patient had a wet dream and came out of the coma.

In the afternoon she had two orderlies at once; all the while, a mini-igloo cooler sat on the nightstand holding a kidney one of them was in the process of delivering. Late in the day, completely consumed by her drive, after the doctor pronounced dead a hall-of-fame basketball player, Maria even shagged the tagged toe.

That night in bed, Dave focused on just riding things out until their appointment with Cynthia the next morning. Maria walked through their bedroom in a slip and a strong, cool wind blew behind. The curtains swayed; Dave shivered as the flames in the fireplace went out. He contemplated donning his miner's head lamp but quickly thought better of it.

They arrived at the office early, only to find Cynthia unabashedly scratching herself. Fortunately, the psychic wasn't a man with both legs on his desk and his head between his legs. Once, Dave had read an intriguing survey in a popular men's magazine stating that two or three men out of a thousand can do that. He remembered being amazed that two or three out of a thousand had tried.

Beginning their consultation with Cynthia, they talked like old friends. Dave jokingly said, "I bet no one has ever come to you wanting you to channel a sheep."

Cynthia named a recent client from Alabama who had spent his whole life in the shadow of his older brother. Distraught at always being second best and wanting to prove himself to his dying father, the man confirmed that it was he, not his brother, who was the Don Juan of that farm. He fought debilitating fatigue working backbreaking hours on the farm, then spent entire nights in the barn. Many a time he almost perished, loosing control of the tractor while reading the Kama Sutra. Client confidentiality was certainly not Cynthia's strong suit.

From Dave's previous visits, he remembered that Cynthia needed some items which Pavlov knew intimately, so he'd brought a hamperfull: Maria's panties and his socks. "Unless," he said to Cynthia, "the source would be better?"

She proceeded to take a few pairs of panties and placed them on her desk. Then, while rubbing two milk bones together, she started to pant. Initially concerned, Dave thought the panting was actually a shortness of breath from her face's proximity to the panties, but he quickly relaxed, accepting her gift for cosmic contact.

Slobbering on her blouse, Cynthia slurred, "Oh my! Oh yes! I think I'm getting something!" Then, in a mechanical, trance-like state, "Heavy breathing, vinyl squeaking — The Ghost of Pornos Past! Heavy breathing, vinyl squeaking — The Ghost of Pornos Past!"

By this time Dave was thinking his money would have been better spent at Hooters. As Cynthia composed herself she said to Maria, "My dear, she's in you." They stood to leave, assuming Cynthia had consumed more than her share of catnip, when she reiterated, "Don't be afraid, but she's in you."

Maria and Dave returned to their seats, and Cynthia's whole body shook violently as sweat flew everywhere. "She's known as The Ghost of Pornos Past, and she's currently residing in your vagina," Cynthia explained uninhibitedly.

Luckily, in this time of cosmic wonderment, Dave kept his mouth shut as he couldn't prevent the thought, "That gives new meaning to the term 'being holed up,'" from rolling through his mind. "Let me get this straight," he said, "there's a ghost occupying Maria's privates?" Panicking, he continued, "Let's get her to the YWCA right away! She could lounge in the sauna until it finds a better host environment."

Cynthia contended that displacing the ghost wouldn't be that simple but speculated there was no reason to worry, as she understood the ghost to be peaceful. Her only effect on Maria would be the tendency towards raging nymphomania.

Gathering himself, Dave deduced, "So what's known as The Ghost of Pornos Past is the spirit of a deceased, female porn star." Increasingly concerned, he continued, "Uh, is she alone? I mean there are a lot of porn stars today who travel with an entourage."

Cynthia smiled, "No, there's no posse in her pussy."

Accepting the situation, Dave sat back and

pondered the circumstances. "Why not?" he thought. After all, he knew countless people whose New York City apartments didn't have much more square footage. It all started making perfect sense, including Pavlov's apparent Tourettish humping.

Cynthia added, "The Ghost of Pornos Past could be peacefully removed through a vaginal exorcism. You may want to try a man of the cloth, as it's very likely the ghost has inhabited the territory expecting it to be a location of eternal piece.

"Vaginal exorcisms are more common in this country than most think. The practice is believed to have originated in the Caribbean where they also began implementing cosmic sexual-manipulation, using what's now popularly referred to as a wedgee board. Vaginal exorcisms aren't unlike traditional ones in that they begin with a lot of yelling and most often end in a cloud of strange-smelling smoke. I know, as I've witnessed this magnificent, liberating process first hand."

Still grasping to absorb this situation, Dave asked Cynthia, "I thought that you could only channel the ghosts of pets?"

"Oh no," she replied, "I can communicate with all ghost beings. There are more similarities between them than one might think." As she spoke, the commonality between a female porn star and a pooch became quite clear. Both spend a considerable amount of time on all fours and are often begging for something; both like a fat guy better if he owns a convertible.

Before calling a priest, Dave considered contacting Ghost Busters. Then he remembered how their efforts had ended in a prodigious sliming incident. Besides, trying to find a priest who has experience with vaginal exorcisms is no easier then finding one who can recommend a good hair-transplant doctor. Most of them probably couldn't even find the vagina, let alone exorcise it.

With Maria consumed by the raging nymphomania caused by The Ghost of Pornos Past, Dave knew it would be up to him to resolve things. At this point Cynthia would be of no help with this process, as she was frantically trying to hide all the long, smooth objects in her office from Maria.

Dave decided he needed to assemble a task force of the most knowledgeable people in the field of libidinous metaphysics. He envisioned creating "The V Team" — immediately, he knew whom to call. Dave phoned Ron Jeremy, the legendary porn star who was in Okinawa autographing his new, latex fist/forearm replicas. Ron responded as if Dave had called from the Make A

Wish Foundation. Eve Ensler, creator and performer of "The Vagina Monologues," flew back from the Congo where she was on tour with the Talking Heads. And Stephen Hawking, renowned, British theoretical physicist, canceled his tanning session when his nurse whispered the info in his ear.

Converged at Dave's apartment, the scene resembled that of Los Alamos in the forties (not a Tex-Mex restaurant in Hell's Kitchen). People mingled, theories flew, and the undeniable feel of historical significance abounded.

Dave overheard Ron talking to Stephen about sitting in his hot tub and seeing a constellation that resembled a woman blowing the Little Dipper, while she took it from behind from the Big Dipper. Stephen's expression brightened as he said, "Ah, the Double Dipper — it is thought to only happen every 1,259.4 years."

As Dave spoke to Eve, he noticed a budding friendship emerging between the physicist and the porn star. Now middle-aged and slightly portly, Ron's mid-section was finally more proportionate to his penile girth.

To meet Ron's posed challenge, Stephen worked frantically to calculate Ron's erectile speed. Velocity = Length + Girth x Pie was the equation formulated. Hawking, confined to a wheelchair by a degenerative muscular disease, communicated this theorem by manipulating his voice synthesizer. Interestingly, when not talking, Ron licked his own arm like a neurotic cat.

Getting the team to focus was a slow and arduous task. Finally Ron proposed, "Why don't I just have sex with Maria?" Not seeing this as the needed solution, Dave stood dumbfounded but, in a way, not completely surprised. Then, with a more convincing argument Ron continued, "I mean, I've probably done her before — not your girlfriend, though I can't say for sure, but the ghost."

Dave wondered, "Could Ron have exhausted the human female pool and now be fornicating with the paranormal and possibly even extraterrestrials?"

Ron continued jokingly, "Doing Maria with the ghost inside would be like double penetration." It was at this point that Dave understood one of Ron's many idiosyncrasies. He wore a shirt with double pockets, chewed Double Mint Gum and was even double-parked outside their building.

Sensing that neither Dave nor Maria, even in her nymphomania state, had embraced his suggestion, Ron returned to his conversation with Stephen. Inquisitively picking up where he'd left off, "If I were on a planet that had no gravity, does that mean I'd have an erection all the time?"

Again, with much difficulty, Dave got the crew to concentrate. It was more challenging than he'd ever imagined as Eve just wanted to see it and talk about it, Ron just wanted to do it, and Stephen just wanted its dimensions.

By accident Dave buzzed up some groupies. When the two middle-aged women entered the apartment, he was intrigued at the one wanting to see Ron and stupefied that the other was there for Stephen. Of all the people on earth to have groupies, it would be one who'd do anybody and another who couldn't.

As Dave was escorting these ladies out the door, he was met by, for what was sure to be the last time, two Jehovah's Witnesses. He offered, "If you want to witness something come on in, you're just in time."

As greater frustration and now hunger set in, Dave regretted not having hired a caterer. Sinking into a comfortable stupor on his futon, he pondered the pending lawsuit from prison by a prolific cannibal against the families of his victims. The convict and his legal counsel contended that his cardiovascular disease was a direct result of the deceased's high-fat content due to their careless and irresponsible lifestyles. One lawyer even threatened to seek manslaughter compensation if his client were to pass prior to execution. Angered at this scenario, Dave contemplated a new paranormal entity, The Ghost of American Character.

Still lounging, he decided to enjoy the playful exchanges continuing between Ron and Stephen. Stephen announced his contention that there were do-able life forms in other solar systems. However, he speculated that anatomically speaking it wouldn't be pleasurable for either party, as their genitalia would be four times the size of an average human's. He then realized his oversight, as this environment would be perfect for Ron.

Dave imagined Ron, en route to a planet in a remote galaxy, saying, "Houston, I have an erection!" Then, exiting the craft, a large bulge in the front of his space suit, Ron blurting, "I'm here to do your leader." Ron and Stephen continued to carry on like old buddies, even divulging their likes of "Star Trek" women.

As Dave sat in a peaceful state, he silently complimented himself on the individuals he'd assembled. He didn't want an exorcism where there were men wearing funny hats, some wearing funny robes and others who had shaved heads or just smelled bad.

Realizing he'd been remiss in not formally introducing his guests, Dave proceeded to do the honors. Before naming Eve, he said "A woman who's made great strides for women and knows a thing or two about the vagina."

"Ah, the founder of Summer's Eve," Ron interjected. Clapping in applause and gratitude, he continued, "She's made great strides for men, too."

He followed with a fascinating tale of an ancestor who had indirectly changed public greetings forever. This fellow had taken it upon himself to walk the streets of London notifying women in need of hygienic assistance. Ron related, "He would cover his nose with his hat and say, 'Bidet, Madam,' which later evolved into the common, polite tip-of-the-hat and 'Good day, Madam.' The gentleman would then depart these encounters with the farewell, 'I bid you a-douche.' "

Eve was quick to clarify the misunderstanding and convey that she was here with immense knowledge of women's relationships to their vaginas, not to perform some industrial-strength douching.

Stephen, now focusing intently on Maria, inquired, "Has stuff been getting pulled up in there, into the area I call The Event Horizon?"

Dave imagined being with Maria in public as

assorted stuff flew towards her vagina — a tablecloth wrapped around her, a poodle lodged against her midsection, and even some unfortunate man's toupee clung to a receptive, lower-abdominal mole. Although Dave was thoroughly apologetic, the man exhausted his patience by using Maria's middle to refit it to his head.

Ron interjected, "All vaginas are magnetic; they all pull stuff towards them. People, objects, you name it, get drawn towards them."

Realizing his wisdom, Dave added, "Yeah, some are even strong enough to pull a Corvette their way."

Digressing again, Ron stated, "I've heard the greatest challenge for audiences at performances of 'The Vagina Monologues' is that once a month the dialogue gets difficult to understand."

Stephen, in a chivalrous attempt to defend Eve's work, piped up, "The London Times said it was a bloody good show!"

Maria, understandably irked at the rest of them, said, "You know what? I think I could learn to live with The Ghost of Pornos Past!"

And with that Dave stood there petrified, quivering as he signed the deliverer's order for Maria's commercial-size generator.

Eve and Ron, arm-in-arm, headed for the door. Ron paused, putting his hand on Dave's shoulder, "If you need to double your extension to reach another dimension — check my website and buy my pills."

Instructions to My Clone

Instructions to My Clone

"Hey studman, it's me. Or you — same difference. Just wanted to give you, well myself, a few recommendations for another time around. Let's say 'you,' but we know what I mean. This way I won't feel like I'm talking to myself.

"I'll keep it simple and go chronologically from the beginning, just in the event my brain copy and download would meet with complications." Dave paused while dictating his recording, pondering existence for a moment.

His recent independent entrepreneurial project had met with some success. As a result, Dave wanted to create a rewarding life for his clone and had gone to great lengths to provide abundant opportunities. He had commissioned a pioneer in deep-sea audio transmission to devise a method of beaming his words into the abdomen, through the amniotic fluid to the fetus. These audio waves could be captured via an inserted, customized diaphragm that could be directed like a satellite dish.

Dave resumed recording, "In addition to my message and depending on the position of the woman carrying you, you will also be able to pick up regional trucker CB's. Should your host get a Brazilian bikini wax and if the weather's right," he speculated, "you might even be able to receive BBC radio.

"Modest beginnings. In the womb things are fairly straightforward and logical — no concerns about avoiding interaction with people who watch reality television or steering clear of those in the process of Dunkin' Donuts assisted suicides."

Dave recalled Dr. Jack Kavorkian commenting that he could have never predicted this mainstream version of his practice. Still puzzled by the deviations from his direct and successful method, he wondered why so many chose to imbibe themselves with low doses of poison provided by giant American food companies and stretch their suicide into a multi-decade event. Leaving dignified suicide to the distinguishing few, these morbidly obese Americans buried themselves under themselves one pound at a time — six feet under, well only three in some places. Who would have guessed that Jim Jones would have his name beside Sara Lee and Betty Crocker.

Continuing the recording, Dave advised, "This uncomplex time in the womb is advantageous, as it will enable you to focus on your Intra-Uterine Training. The I.U.T. is a system of prenatal conditioning exercises done in the womb using miniature, collapsible workout equipment called the GYN/GYM, an invention I've patented for your benefit. The I.U.T. is designed to advance by trimester. Don't be concerned about doing these exercises without a jockstrap, as your balls haven't dropped yet. However, I've designed a weightlifting belt with disposable diaper attachments for your post-natal workouts.

"You don't want to wait until you're two, like Tiger Woods, to start training. By the time you're born, that kind of delay would be career catastrophe, as some athletes are now over-the-hill in their mid-teens. For many, pubescence means it's time to start coaching a girls' volleyball team in Omaha. Those who can extend their careers often celebrate with a sports-retirement/sweet-sixteen party.

"Besides, as a toddler one requires a sophisticated training team consisting of a nutritionist, strength and conditioning coach, chiropractor and psychologist. Whereas all you need with the I.U.T.

regimen is a gynecologist who can throw a medicine ball.

"The time during your third trimester will be your introduction to extreme sports. You can build nerves of steel umbilical-cord bungee jumping and develop superior reflexes on the fallopian-tube luge. When your surrogate's water breaks, you will be capable of surfing out to avoid the trauma of labor.

"Did I forget to mention — you are a clone. The woman who is carrying you is not your biological mother, so feel free to take liberties with the breast feeding. I've paid her handsomely to pump breast milk between feedings to be mixed in a blender with protein powder for supplemental bodybuilding shakes. She's also been trained to change your diaper without interrupting your abdominal crunches.

"Avoid addiction to violent video games as, unlike some of your peers, you can be free of carpal tunnel syndrome and the urge to murder large groups of people. Instead, engage in exercise and eat well to avoid developing allergies so abundant that they include everything except products made in Hershey, Pennsylvania or in strict adherence with the Colonel's recipes. Who wants a scene where they can't grip their emergency asthma inhaler due to the chicken fat on their fingers?

"Girls! Here I don't know whether to throw up my hands and say, 'Sorry I can't help you,' or record an additional eight hours. For whatever it's worth, I'll give it a shot and touch on this in all the future sections. But for starters, don't be the guy only trying to get into a girl's pants to see if they have exact change for the Pepsi machine. The girls will have been exposed to massive quantities of hormones in their diet and will greatly exceed your maturity, now and forever. The only thing some men will do is close the gap.

"As you age, you'll blossom into puberty. Now, you don't want to be sent to the school nurse's station to submit to DNA testing to see if you're the new father in Homeroom 400. So let's see if I can come up with some solutions. If I were to recommend the withdrawal method, I would have to say that, unless you've recently watched a clone of Al Roaker give the weather, anything over five seconds is pushing it. Better yet, make friends with the Monica Lewinski clone.

"It will be tough, as you'll be in great demand to your female classmates, since the majority of your male counterparts will be suffering from prepubescent adult-type diabetes, frequently causing impotence. It's not likely that they will ever be able to engage beyond heavy petting. The girls are going to want to play doctor and most of the boys will need to see one.

"Academically, the only competition will come from other clones and Orientals, whom you won't be able to tell whether they're clones or not. But not to worry, because my generous donations will keep collegiate doors open. Also, some of your friends will have severe attention deficit disorder. However, it never manifests when they're eating, so this is the time to discuss homework.

"In sports there are many things to be wary of, for instance the girl playing on the boys' soccer team. She'll be short, stocky but very fast, her parents from an Eastern Bloc country. She'll seem sweet enough, but get in a skirmish with her for the ball in the far corner of the field and, as the ninety-year-old ref makes a feigned attempt to run down the field, you'll be getting kicked in the nuts and poked in the eyes.

"When in high school, be on the lookout for horny and available teachers. This is a time in your life when doing older women is desirable. There might be a kinky French teacher who wants to role play WWII and have you invade from the east, all the while doing something strange with a baguette from the west. Steer clear of the lunch ladies though, as I know a hairnet with garters attaching it to fishnet stockings isn't quite as erotic in person as in fantasy. Besides, during foreplay, the aroma of burnt macaroni and cheese isn't the aphrodisiac it may be to some of your classmates.

"No hesitation should occur in fornicating with other students' moms. This is merely an anthropological investigation which you can consider as taking a personal interest in where they came from. Have free roam of the liquor cabinet while she takes a dustmop to her privates, as single moms often can't find time to date. It's like the room at your grandparents' house that's a bit too tidy and always smells funny.

"I'm out of time for now, but will pick up where I left off later. As always, my parting instructions are: religiously carry a Henry Miller book, and realize that cloning yourself is a bad idea — you're insane!"

Who Wants to be Blake Richards' Drycleaner?

Who Wants to be Blake Richards' Drycleaner?

Dave sat on the can, a look of deadpan, in his room at the Embassy Suites. He hated to travel and tremored when he flew. His consolation was relaxing in the fully loaded heads of upscale hotels. When in his room and not asleep in his bed, all Dave's time was spent there. He played solitaire, called his cousin, and ordered bathroom food service. He even ingeniously used the tile floor and a round bar of hotel soap for games of shuffleboard.

Normally Dave's TV viewing consisted of pay-per-view movies (mainly old spaghetti westerns) and infomercials of women selling exercise equipment or tanning lotions. He found it very soothing to watch women abolishing their pale cellulite for golden brown muscle. But today he decided to deviate from his regimen and channel-surf on the TV visible through the open bathroom door.

One of Dave's many idiosyncrasies was that instead of using hotel toilet paper, he always brought his own from home. Having heard too many urban legends relating to prankster housekeepers, he didn't take any chances. As he sat atop his rented throne, fortunately not accompanied by any jesters, he browsed the channels. He was stupefied by the reality TV fad that had consumed the country in recent years. With every passing day and yet another creativity homicide, one more time slot filled with an even dumber reality show. Dave had never watched these shows as he'd fallen ill even from brief exposure to their promos. Being in a bathroom that he was not responsible for was the only place he might dare venture into this kind of viewing.

Suddenly, Dave's button-pushing thumb froze, temporarily paralyzed like his now-numb legs as he had forgotten to do his hourly yoga. Had his legs and hand fallen asleep from a pinched nerve, or had he had a stroke? Dave's thoughts immediately turned to Elvis. He wondered if he, too, would die seated, and was it the location of the great rocker's demise that led to his title of The King?

While he catatonically gazed at the screen, being the top of the hour, the programming changed. A modified Tom Jones tune began playing as theme music. As text flashed on the screen, a voiceover that sounded like Marv Albert said, "Who Wants to be Blake Richards' Drycleaner?" Dave panicked as he thought he actually must have had a stroke and this was his brain's misinterpretation. But the introduction continued, and he soberly accepted it as another giant step backward for mankind. Only vaguely familiar with these shows, Dave speculated it might be some strange mix of "Fear Factor" and "Survivor."

The announcer continued, "These six men and six women are competing to see who gets to be Blake Richards' drycleaner! We cut these twelve contestants loose on the streets of New York City. After thirty days, the person who has corralled and personally dry-cleaned the most bike messengers' clothes will prove that they are ultimately worthy of the ultimate dry-cleaning honor."

Dave thought, "This might be entertaining; those messengers change flat tires more often than they change their spandex shorts."

The show's opener included a replay of a couple of the chosen contestants' audition tapes. The first tape showed a crazed man looting jockstraps and socks from a men's locker room and then sprinting down the front steps of a YMCA, arms loaded with bounty. Another, featuring the international field of competitors, showed a woman sitting calmly in a dimly lit room smoking a cigarette. She confidently stated, "I was the sumo wardrobe director in Japan. I spent years processing the thongs of four hundred pound men."

The unseen host proceeded, "Here's what happened on the first nine days en route to finding the grand champion of launderers. Tim, the self-proclaimed King of All Swingers Clubs Towel Boys, was disqualified on day two for hamper tampering. Then on day six, Sue and Bob formed an alliance that soon thereafter blossomed into a romance." The host concluded, "After the break, we'll pick up the action on day ten!"

As the commercials for other reality shows ran, Dave's attention wandered after the one titled "Afgan's Barber." As he glanced around his tile abode, the 24-pack of Regal toilet paper, which he always brought on his travels, caught his eye. On the side of the wrapping uninhibitedly stood an 800 number and the words, "Questions or Comments." Perplexed and simultaneously scared, Dave contemplated this sighting, incapable of comprehending that anyone could have either. Even if they did, he thought, they wouldn't be brazen enough to call. Had he been at home, he would have been too self-conscious to dial. On the road, though, Dave had no concerns about his foreign-exchange senior citizen listening on another phone or the telephone company monitoring his activity. Fortunately, a racy Bally Total Fitness commercial had returned mobility to all his appendages, enabling his operation of the bathroom phone.

⇨ "Welcome to the Regal toilet tissue customer service line:
For English, press 1.
Für Deutsch, trücken sie 2."

Dave pressed 1 and for the first time was actually quite relieved to encounter an automated system.

⇨ "If this is an emergency, please press
the # key now for direct connection
to our 24-hour hotline."

Dave anxiously awaited the menu options.

⇨ "If you are calling regarding our recent recall, please press 1."

Concerned, as he'd been a loyal brand customer but not a CNN banner reader, Dave contemplated pressing 1. However, being that he'd already used a dozen rolls, he decided that, like any case of Old Milwaukee, once you're half into it there's no turning back.

His philosophizing was interrupted by:

➩ "If you are a plaintiff in the pending class action suit, please press 2."

The reality show returned with the camera focused on Marv Albert standing at the bottom of a laundry chute, knee-deep in clothes, casually sifting through them. "We're back on day 10! In the event the contest should end in a tie, there will be a one-day playoff to determine the winner. The playoff's rules will be the same, but instead of obtaining bike messengers' clothes, the contestants have to acquire NYC cab drivers' attire."

Dave pondered this challenge in the seconds before the next telephone prompt:

➩ "For Regal-related health information, please press 3."

Dave pressed 3, now always fearing that he may not be fully up-to-date on the latest findings and recommendations. He remembered arriving in Hong Kong on one of his business trips in the midst of the SARS epidemic and mistaking the masked pandemonium for their national Michael Jackson Day. In hindsight, Dave wondered if Michael's wearing a surgical mask was a preventative measure for his interaction with monkeys. Dave remembered, vividly, the long walk home to his hotel, his surgical mask recycling his breath after dining at an all-you-can-eat sushi buffet.

He'd felt bad for locals who'd taken the greatest economic hits: the working girls, as it had put a big dent in their oral sex trade, and the spa employees, since women were no longer having their upper lips and chins waxed.

The Regal health options began:

➩ "If you're Kosher, please press 1.
For use at high altitudes, please press 2.
Or select 9 to return to the main menu."

Dave chose 9. He waited morbidly as the recording recycled through the previous options to the following prompt:

➩ "If you'd like to see your face printed on
our special customer-edition rolls, please
press number 4."

Dave thought about how many people he wanted to kiss his ass, and now he just needed their pictures.

His mind wandered from both the telephone and the television as he berated himself about his last trip to New York City. He'd made the mistake of allowing himself to be talked into taking a bicycle rickshaw from JFK airport into Manhattan. The only time saved by taking one of these now-popular pedicabs was not getting held up at traffic lights by hobos squeegeing your windshield. He had calculated the reduction in air-resistance time gained by choosing the driver with the smallest turban, but had been unable to foresee the delay caused when the driver rear-ended a police horse.

Refocusing his attention for a moment on the reality show, Dave witnessed a frantic contestant working from a makeshift, shopping-cart dry-cleaning rig that he'd attached to a fire hydrant, improvisationally ironing a pair of bike shorts right on a bicycle seat.

The voice in Dave's phone ear prompted:

⇨ "If you wish to speak with a customer service representative, please stay on the line. Due to our unusually high volume of calls, the current waiting time is twenty-seven minutes."

As the on-hold music began, its rhythm was occasionally interrupted by the following public service announcement:

⇨ "If you or someone close to you has become a compulsive toilet paper user, there is help. Check our online support group at www.regal.com/clean. Hear stories of others who have now been clean for years."

While the on-hold music continued, Dave

wondered what clinically qualified someone as a compulsive user. Was there a checklist of tell-tale addictive habits, such as:

- No longer using Regal only socially.
- Trading sexual favors for toilet paper.
- A history of toilet tissue use in your family.
- Using toilet tissue just to fit in.

While Dave speculated, the recording continued to cycle monotonously. A voice finally interrupted:

➩ "This is Melissa, your personal, automated representative. Please answer the following questions to let me know how I may help you. If at any time during our conversation you want to go back to the previous question, say, 'Go Back.' "

Dave, a devout detester of this kind of customer service practice, blurted, "Get off my back!"

Melissa:

➩ "I'm sorry, I didn't understand that. To help me find a specific answer to your question, please define the product you're calling about with terms like one-ply or extra absorbency."

"Osso buco!" Dave shouted.

Melissa:

➪ "I do not understand what you said.
Please use words like crap or dumping."

"Stopped-up!" Dave interjected.

Melissa:

➪ "You said, 'Gift shop.' Tell me what items you'd be interested in ordering, after I mention the following selections.

"Or, to transfer into the Regal International Singles' chat line, say, 'Unoccupied.'"

Dave, no longer capable of resisting, uttered, "Unoccupied." He had immediate fantasies of being at dinner parties with his new love, anxiously awaiting others asking the inevitable question, "So, where'd you two meet?"

➪ "Welcome to the Regal International Singles' chat line," a sexy voice extended.

Dave poised himself as he was green to this game. He thought about opening strong with, "What are you wearing pushed down to your ankles?"

The sultry intro continued enticingly:

➪ "Apply now to be a participant on our upcoming, premier reality show, 'Shitmates.'

> Join another sassy single on a blind date aboard our cruise ship touring third-world ports. We'll equip you with backpacks filled with Regal, so that you can explore, drink the water, and hopefully find true love."

Dave somberly hung up the phone, turned off the television and rose from his seat. He pulled up his pants, didn't bother to button them and retrieved some money from his pocket. As he left a hefty tip on the tank, his pants fell back to his feet. Dave morosely waddled to the balcony and, with much difficulty, climbed over the rail. Dozens of street onlookers now gazed upward. Without hesitation he jumped, plummeting eighty feet to his death.

As the spectators began to disperse, a twelve-year-old girl said to her friend, "That was pretty good! This show will make it, but I still like 'The Bachelor' better."